Lift the Stigma PH

Written by: Francis Louie Ramoso

For permission requests, contact:
Francis Louie C. Ramoso
Barangay Agay-ayan, Gingoog City, 9014, Philippines
Email: louiewoodlegacy@gmail.com

First Edition
Published by LOUIEWOOD, Philippines
Distributed worldwide through major and local publishing platforms.

LOUIEWOOD *is the official publishing imprint of Francis Louie C. Ramoso.*

ISBN: 978-621-06-3233-0

Preface

This book is not just about cannabis. It's about truth, discrimination, corruption, and the voices that have been silenced for too long in the Philippines. "Lift The Stigma PH" is a movement — a message from the unheard, the criminalized, the misunderstood. My name is Francis Louie, and like many others, I've lived through judgment, fear, confusion, and the weight of a broken system. But I also believe in hope. In healing. In revolution — one led by truth.

If you're holding this book, you're already part of the fight. Let's raise our voices together.

Epigraph

"This is not just about a plant. It's about the right to heal, to rise, and to be heard." — Anonymous Filipino Voice

Dedication

To our ancestors who knew the power of plants, and to the next generation who will reclaim it. May your minds stay open, your spirits stay strong, and your healing be your revolution.

Introduction

"This is bigger than a plant."
In the Philippines, saying the word "marijuana" out loud still gets side-eyes, whispers, or worse — handcuffs. For decades, we've been told it's evil. A gateway drug. A sin. A crime.
But behind that fear is something deeper: A war not just on a plant — but on truth, healing, and freedom.
This book isn't here to glorify cannabis. It's here to humanize the people whose lives have been crushed, judged, or erased because of it. It's here to ask the questions no one dares to ask:
Why is something that can heal being treated like poison?
Who benefits from keeping it illegal?
Why are the poor punished while the powerful profit?
And what does justice really look like in a country that criminalizes survival?
Cannabis has always been part of human history — including ours. Long before colonizers set foot on this land, Filipino healers already understood its power. But that story was buried. Stigmatized. Twisted by fear, foreign laws, and political control.
What you're about to read is not just a collection of facts — it's a challenge to look deeper. To question what you were taught. To listen to the voices that have been silenced. To lift the stigma — and begin a national healing.
You don't have to be a user to care. You just have to be human.
Because this is no longer just about cannabis. This is about justice, truth, and the future of the Philippines.

Table of Contents

✍ Author's Note

I didn't write this book to be famous. I wrote it because I've seen too much, felt too much, and stayed silent for too long.

I've seen good people locked up, judged, or buried — not because they were criminals, but because the system was never built to understand them. I've seen mothers cry, fathers break, and youth lose their way — all while the truth was hidden behind laws, lies, and power plays.

What you'll find in these pages is truth, plain and simple.

Sometimes uncomfortable. Sometimes painful. Always necessary.

This book is for those who don't have a mic. For those who were told to shut up, clean up, and disappear. For those who turned to cannabis for relief, and got a case instead of care. For every Filipino who's been told that healing is a crime.

I'm not a politician. I'm not a doctor. I'm just a voice — one of many — rising from the ground up.

And if this book can help start a conversation, shift a mindset, or plant a seed that grows into change… then every word was worth it.

The movement doesn't start in Congress or in courts. It starts with us — in the streets, in our stories, and in our hearts.

Thank you for picking this up. For reading with an open mind. And most of all, for daring to imagine something better.

— Francis Louie

2025, somewhere in the Philippines, where truth still burns bright.

Chapter 1: The Stigma

The Stigma

In the Philippines, the word "marijuana" doesn't just raise eyebrows — it **raises walls**. Walls between families. Walls between truth and lies. Walls that divide people into "good" or "bad" — just because of a plant.

Say "marijuana" in a crowded jeepney and feel the air shift. Watch eyes dart. Listen to the silence. It's not just a word — it's a **verdict**, a **sentence**, a **label**. Addict. Criminal. Lazy. Rebel. "Wala nang pag-asa 'yan." These are not facts — they are judgments. Born not out of understanding, but out of fear. And fear, when repeated enough, becomes **culture**.

But here's the truth: the fear is not ours. It was **taught** to us. Passed down like a curse from generations of colonization, corruption, and control.

The Lie We Were Sold

For decades, the Filipino people have been spoon-fed the idea that marijuana is evil. From classroom lectures to Sunday sermons, from police announcements to morning radio — the message was clear: "Masama 'yan. Iwasan mo 'yan. Makukulong ka d'yan."

But no one told us *why*. No one questioned *who* was behind this message, or what they were gaining from it.

What if the real danger wasn't the plant — but the story we've been told about it?

Personal Story: Tito Ben

Let me tell you about **Tito Ben**.

He wasn't a criminal. He wasn't an addict. He was a farmer. A father. A kind soul. After his wife died of breast cancer, he tried everything to manage his own stress and chronic pain. The meds the doctor gave made him weak, dizzy, and broke. So, like many others in the provinces, he turned to cannabis. Grew a little. Used a little.

One night, police raided his home. No warrant. No questions. Just boots, guns, and accusations. They called him a "drug personality" on TV. Neighbors stopped talking to his children. His name was destroyed in a day. He's still in jail today — for what? A handful of dried leaves.

Meanwhile, politicians in the capital steal millions with a smile.

That's not justice. That's a **war on the poor**.

Why the Fear Persists

Let's be real: **stigma is profitable**.

Media companies earn by feeding fear. Politicians score points with "tough on crime" speeches. Law enforcement fills quotas. Private jails rake in money. Pharmaceutical companies lobby to keep alternatives illegal.

And we? The people? We get silence. We get shame. We get afraid of each other.

The Language of Judgment

We need to talk about the words we use.

"Baliw."
"Adik."
"Walang kwenta."
"Sayang ka."

These words kill more dreams than drugs ever could. These are the weapons used in our homes, schools, barangays. And sometimes, we don't even realize we're passing the curse forward.

Ask yourself: Have I ever judged someone for using? Have I ever looked down on someone because of what I heard, not what I knew?

If the answer is yes, you're not alone — but now is the time to unlearn.

Stigma is Deadly

People die not because they used cannabis — they die because they were too scared to ask for help.

- Cancer patients suffer in silence, denied access to natural pain relief.
- Young boys are locked up, branded as criminals, just for experimenting.
- Breadwinners lose jobs. Kids lose parents. Families fall apart.

And yet, **none of this is happening in countries where cannabis is legal**. They moved forward. We stayed stuck — in fear, in pride, in silence.

Reflection Box

"When was the first time you heard that cannabis was 'bad'? Who told you? Have you ever questioned that belief?"

Write your answers below. No shame. Just honesty.

Truth vs. System

The system that criminalizes cannabis is the same system that **protects abusers, jails the poor**, and **silences the brave**.

It's not a system built on truth — it's built on fear and control. And it thrives when we don't ask questions.

But this generation is waking up. We are asking. We are challenging. And we are no longer afraid to say: **The system is broken.**

Healing is Not a Crime

I've seen mothers hiding the truth from their children. I've seen sick people choosing pain over prison. I've seen families crumble because they were too scared to tell their neighbors the truth.

But I've also seen **hope**.

I've seen people heal. I've seen stories shift. I've seen youth speak up. And I've seen that when the stigma is lifted — even just a little — people breathe easier.

Because cannabis is not the enemy.

The enemy is **ignorance**.
The enemy is **greed**.
The enemy is **shame**.

And the only cure is **truth**.

Call to Arms 🚨

This chapter is your wake-up call. Your reminder. Your challenge.

Do not let fear rule your beliefs. Do not let lies define your truth. Question everything. Speak up. Listen. And most of all — **fight for those who can't**.

Because lifting the stigma isn't just about weed.

It’s about **justice**.
It’s about **freedom**.
It’s about **compassion**.
It’s about **us**.

Let’s lift it — together. 🩶
One story at a time. One truth at a time. One chapter at a time.

Chapter 2: The Real Enemy

They told us cannabis was the enemy.

They printed it in textbooks.
Preached it from pulpits.
Blasted it over radios.
Pushed it in classrooms with puppet teachers reading from broken scripts.
They showed us mugshots of skinny boys, dazed eyes, plastic sachets — and called them "threats."
But they never showed us the ones in power.

Because here's the truth:

The real enemy doesn't smell like weed — it reeks of power.

It wears suits, not slippers.
It hides behind podiums, not corners.
It signs bills with one hand and steals futures with the other.

The System They Built

Let's stop pretending this is about "safety."

If this war on drugs was really about safety,

- Why are our jails filled with kids and not cartels?
- Why are the sick still dying waiting for medicine?
- Why are rehab centers underfunded, while prisons overflow?

The system was **never built to protect**.
It was built to **control**.

And cannabis? It threatens control.

Why?

Because cannabis heals the poor **without a prescription.**
Because it grows freely **without a patent.**
Because it opens minds **without permission.**

That's terrifying to a system that survives on obedience.

Layers of the Enemy

1. Politicians Who Preach but Don't Practice
They hold press cons about moral values, then party with drug lords behind closed doors.
They pass laws against addiction while addicted to greed and applause.

2. Corporations Who Profit from Sickness
Pharmaceutical giants would rather you buy painkillers every month than grow one plant in your backyard.
Cannabis doesn't make them rich — so they lobby to keep it illegal.

3. Law Enforcement Chained by Quotas
Policemen are pressured to produce arrests — not justice.
They chase kids with joints while smugglers ride convoys unchecked.

4. Media That Sells Fear
Every headline screams "DRUG SUSPECT KILLED" — no trial, no context, no name.
Why? Because fear sells. And silence pays more.

Real Story: "Arnold" from Quezon City

Arnold was 19. His father was bedridden.
He started buying weed for his dad's chronic back pain — just a few sticks, nothing serious.
One night, he got caught in a buy-bust. No gun. No syndicate ties.

Just a boy, a budget, and some hope.
Now he's facing years. First-time offense, no violent record, no bail.

Meanwhile, the barangay captain rumored to be selling meth from his backyard?
Promoted.
Endorsed by a senator.
Even got a project named after him.

This is not war. This is genocide. One joint at a time.

The Silence of the "Good Ones"

Some say, "Not all cops are bad."
"Not all politicians are corrupt."

True. But silence is complicity.

Where are the good ones when the poor are being shot on sight?
Where are the good ones when med students get expelled for cannabis use, but influencers get high on camera and walk free?

The real enemy is not just corruption.
It's the culture of **cover-up** and **cowardice**.

Reflection Box 📓

"Have you ever been afraid to speak the truth because of who might be listening? What would you say if fear wasn't holding you back?"

Write it down. Say it aloud. Don't censor yourself — not here.

The Enemy of Healing

Imagine a Philippines where cannabis is regulated.
Imagine the money saved from unnecessary arrests.

Imagine cancer patients smiling without pain.
Imagine farmers planting legally, selling, thriving.

That world is possible.

But the **enemy fears healing**, because healing leads to power.
And they don't want a powerful people.
They want a **punished** people.
A **divided** people.
A **silent** people.

We Are Not Blind Anymore

The youth are not dumb.
The poor are not voiceless.
The artists, the writers, the farmers, the sick — we all see it now.

We see the raids.
We see the lies.
We see the numbers that don't add up.

And we're done pretending.
We are done apologizing for seeking truth, for demanding justice, for wanting a better future.

Because **anger mixed with clarity?** That's no longer rebellion.
That's revolution.

Call to Action 🚨

Let this be our line in the sand:

We will **no longer fear a system built to exploit us.**
We will name names.
We will write truths.
We will lift each other.

Because if we don't name the **real enemy**,
we'll keep locking up healers, while the true criminals drink cocktails on yachts.

We don't fear the plant.
We fear the silence.

But not anymore.

This Is Our Voice on the Record

To the farmers growing for love — we see you.
To the parents praying for access — we hear you.
To the youth pushing back against fear — we believe in you.

The plant is not the threat.

The real threat is what happens when good people stay quiet.

So speak.
Write.
March.
Vote.
Heal.
Create.
Live.

Let this book be **our proof** that we're not afraid anymore.

Chapter 3: Voices from the Ground

"Wala naman akong pinapatay. Gusto ko lang mawala 'yung sakit."
— **Lolo Arman**, 67, arthritis patient using cannabis oil in secret

---

The Forgotten Majority

They never interview people like us.

There are no microphones in our homes.
No cameras in our pain.
No hashtags for our healing.

In every press conference, the "war on drugs" is framed like a blockbuster: heroes in uniform, villains behind bars. But reality isn't a movie. It's messier, grayer, and deeply human.

Behind every headline, there's a grandmother crying in silence.
A child waking up from another seizure.
A father who risks everything to bring relief home.

This chapter isn't about theory. It's about *testimony.*
This isn't protest. This is *plea.*
These are the stories the system erases.

And it's time we remember them — with names, places, pain, and truth.

Lolo Arman – The Silent Healer

Bukidnon's air is fresh, but Lolo Arman's joints haven't felt peace in years.
Decades in the rice fields took their toll — long days bent under

the sun, carrying sacks of grain, lifting beyond his limits just to put food on the table.

Now, at 67, he spends most days sitting quietly outside his nipa hut, watching birds cross the sky as the ache creeps up his back.

There are no hospitals nearby. Even if there were, he couldn't afford the check-up fee, let alone the medicine.

His 19-year-old grandson, *Jeric*, refused to watch him suffer.
"I read somewhere on Facebook na may gumaling sa langis ng marijuana," he said.
So Jeric learned to make it — carefully, secretly. They grew three wild plants behind the banana trees. No one knows. They can't risk it.

Each night, Lolo rubs the thick oil on his knees. The pain doesn't vanish, but the shaking stops. He sleeps now — which is all he really wants.

"I'm not doing anything wrong," he whispers. "But if they find out, they won't arrest me — they'll take my grandson. That's what I'm afraid of."

In a just world, Jeric would be praised.
Here, he's one call away from being labeled a criminal.

Rosalie – A Mother's Secret

Cavite is noisy, crowded, alive — but for Rosalie, the world has become a slow ticking bomb.

Her son, *Liam*, is eight. His seizures started three years ago — violent spasms that come without warning. She counted every one: 12 in a month, then 20, then 30.
They tried three medications — the cheapest was still ₱900 a bottle. Nothing worked.

Until she met *Tita Carol*, a quiet caregiver from a Facebook group. She offered a small vial of CBD oil. "Subukan mo lang," she said. "Walang halong kemikal."

She tried it.

Within two weeks, Liam's seizures dropped to two per month.

Rosalie cried when she realized it was working — not just tears of joy, but of guilt, fear, rage. Because now she was doing something illegal just to keep her son alive.

"Hindi ako adik," she says, eyes steady. "Nanay ako. And I will protect my child even if the law calls me a criminal."

She hides the oil in an old cough syrup bottle. Not because she's ashamed — but because **love in this country requires secrecy**.

Jay – The Farmer Who Got Caught

In the mountains of Kalinga, *Jay* learned how to plant cannabis from his father. And his father before him. It was never about rebellion — it was tradition, survival, livelihood.

Unlike commercial farming, cannabis needed no pesticide, no irrigation system. It grew wild, resilient, high in the misty slopes. The money it brought paid for school supplies, clothes, medicine.

Jay never smoked. Never even tasted it.

But in 2022, a military operation raided his land. He ran. His wife screamed. His youngest son watched as they burned the only plants that kept them alive.

Jay couldn't afford bail.
He never saw a lawyer.
His only crime was *poverty in the wrong industry.*

Now he's in prison — while businessmen overseas open "Cannabis Startups" with million-dollar investors.

"Kung mayaman ako, legal sana. Pero mahirap lang kami, kaya kulong."

Jay's story is not isolated.
It's the pattern — a system that punishes survival if it doesn't wear a suit.

Martin – I'm Not Broken

In a cramped apartment near Cubao, *Martin* writes songs in a notebook with torn pages.
He's 22. Queer. Scarred by trauma from childhood abuse.

He tried seeing a psychiatrist once — the fee alone drained his monthly savings.
He tried the pills: antidepressants, antipsychotics, anti-everything.
They made him numb, confused, zombie-like.

But when a friend offered a puff of weed one night, something shifted.
The shaking stopped. The voices quieted. He slept for the first time in days.

Martin is not a stereotype.

He's not the loud stoner in your jokes.
He's the quiet student who always showed up.
The cousin who writes poems.
The friend who just wants to feel peace.

"I'm not trying to escape reality," he says. "I'm just trying to survive it."

He's not broken. He's adapting — the only way he knows how.

The Underground Angels

Scattered across the islands are people who don't ask for fame — just space to help.

- In **Davao**, a midwife secretly grows CBD plants to aid elderly cancer patients in her barangay. She doesn't charge. She just can't bear to watch them cry in pain.
- In **Baguio**, a retired teacher puts drops of cannabis oil in her father's morning tea. He has Parkinson's. She calls it "vitamin hope."
- In **Mindoro**, a tricycle driver wraps weed in old candy wrappers. Not to sell, but to soothe his wife's fibromyalgia during flare-ups.

They aren't doctors.
They aren't trained.
They don't need to be.

They are healers — because in a country where healing is illegal, compassion becomes revolution.

Silenced by Fear, United by Compassion

What binds all these stories isn't addiction — it's **love**.

The kind of love that makes you risk everything.
That makes you break unjust laws just to honor your child's dignity.
That keeps you awake at night not from guilt — but from **fear of being caught loving the wrong way**.

This country teaches you that love must follow rules.
But what if the rules are broken?
What if the law forgot who it was meant to serve?

These people — our people — aren't breaking the law.
The law is breaking them.

These Are Not Just Stories — They Are Mirrors

Look closely.

You might see someone who reminds you of your uncle.
Your lola.
Your best friend.
Or maybe even… *you.*

They are not criminals.
They are Filipinos.
And maybe — just maybe — they are also **heroes in disguise.**

✊ Reflection & Call to Action

💭 Have you ever met someone like Lolo Arman? Rosalie? Jay? Martin?
Or maybe you are them — quietly surviving in a system that wants you silent.

🔥 Write your own story. Say it out loud. Post it anonymously. Share it in whispers.

One voice can spark a ripple. A hundred can start a movement.

Let this be our vow: We will not be silent anymore.

Chapter 4: A History of Healing

"Bago pa dumating ang batas, nandito na ang lunas."
— Old Filipino proverb, reawakened

Before the Bans, There Was Balance

Before the world told us what to outlaw,
Before we were taught to fear leaves and flowers,
We were people of the earth — guided not by lawbooks, but by intuition, connection, and ancestral memory.

Cannabis — before it became a slur, a charge, a sentence — was simply part of life.
A leaf. A remedy. A quiet companion in moments of pain, anxiety, and transformation.

It didn't need a warning label.
It didn't need government approval.
It simply needed to grow — and be respected.

This chapter is not just about what we lost.
It's about what we always had — and what we must now reclaim.

🌱 Pre-Colonial Wisdom: Nature as Pharmacy

The first doctors on these islands were not trained in universities — they were babaylans, katalonas, albularyos, and hilots.
Most were women, midwives, shamans, and spiritual leaders.

They held knowledge passed down orally through generations — plant lore, chants, rituals, and sacred relationships with the earth.

Among the hundreds of native medicinal plants known to our ancestors, **cannabis (locally called "kanapi" or "ganja" in some indigenous dialects)** was believed to be used for:

- **Ritual transitions** (births, death rites, dream states)
- **Muscle pain and inflammation**
- **Digestive or respiratory ailments**
- **Mental balancing and calming the soul**

They didn't isolate the mind from the body.
They didn't overpathologize emotions.
To feel too much — sadness, fear, even visions — wasn't always an illness. It was a call for realignment.

And that realignment often came through nature.

"Kung may sakit, may gamot. Kung may gamot, may halaman. Kung may halaman, may Diyos."

Healing wasn't seen as defiance. It was **communion.**

✝ Spanish Era: Colonization and Suppression of Knowledge

When the Spanish arrived in 1521, so began the colonization not just of land — but of memory.

With the cross came the sword, and with the sword came a new order.
Babaylans were labeled witches.
Herbalists became heretics.
Spiritual healers were forced into silence, driven underground, or worse — burned, converted, erased.

Cannabis, along with other native practices, was demonized quietly.
Not necessarily outlawed immediately — but devalued.
Its **sacred status** was stripped and **recast as superstition.**

The friars brought their own "approved" medicines, European botanical texts, and doctrine-heavy medicine tied to obedience and divine punishment.

Still, in the *lihim ng mga barrio*, the old ways endured:

- Leaves were still brewed quietly in clay pots.
- Prayers were still whispered to the diwata.
- Oils were massaged into aching backs, far from the church bells.

A grandmother in Ilocos. A healer in Antique. A father in Zamboanga.
They remembered.

In their kitchens and forest walks, **cannabis survived**.
Not loudly — but stubbornly.

US The American Occupation: From Healing to Criminality

Then came another empire — and this one brought a new weapon: **prohibition.**

In the early 1900s, during American occupation, the U.S. exported not just their education system and politics — but their **moral panic**.

Back in the U.S., marijuana was being used as a scapegoat for xenophobic fears — especially targeting Mexican immigrants and Black Americans. It was portrayed as a drug that caused madness, violence, and moral decay.

This fear campaign was globalized.
By the **1930s**, American law had already criminalized cannabis.
By the **1950s**, it was illegal in the Philippines.
And by **1972**, under Ferdinand Marcos and Martial Law, cannabis became punishable by long-term imprisonment — even death in some cases.

"Hindi mo na pwedeng hawakan ang halamang nakagaling sa'yo — dahil may hawak sa'yo ang batas."

This marked a dramatic shift.

Cannabis wasn't just *ignored* anymore. It was *hunted.*
Possession meant raids.
Usage meant prison.
Farming meant poverty and danger.

And yet — the people never let go.

🔥 But the People Remembered

The heart of a nation doesn't beat in courtrooms.
It beats in its households, farms, and prayers.

Even during the most intense crackdowns, Filipino families continued to turn to cannabis as medicine. It remained a remedy for:

- **Epileptic seizures** in children
- **Chronic pain** in farmers and laborers
- **Depression and trauma** in survivors
- **Insomnia** in the elderly
- **Cancer pain** in the terminally ill

It didn't disappear.
It just changed form:

- Tea instead of tincture
- Oils hidden in old lotion bottles
- Leaves tucked between Bible pages
- Smoke shared not in parties — but in midnight whispers of pain relief

"Ang ipinagbabawal na gamot ay gamot pa rin sa mga nagdurusa. Ipinagbawal lang ito, pero hindi ito nawala."

These were not criminals.
They were healers in exile.
Victims of a government that forgot its own soil.

😨 Cultural Paradoxes: Fear and Forgetting

Here lies the tragic irony:
We glorify herbalism — yet vilify one of the most healing herbs known to man.

We boast of *sambong*, *tanglad*, *pandan*, and *lagundi*.
We export *malunggay capsules* to other countries.

But mention cannabis — and suddenly, the tone shifts:

- "Addict ka?"
- "Masama yan!"
- "Ikukulong ka diyan!"

Why?

Because our **memory was colonized.**
We inherited the fears of foreigners — and forgot our own courage.

Because the systems that taught us health didn't come to heal — they came to **control**.

🧠 Rediscovery in the Age of Information

But the winds are changing.

We live in an age where information can't be burned, buried, or banned.

- Young Filipinos are questioning the narratives they inherited.
- Farmers are revisiting old planting traditions.
- Academics are researching pre-colonial medicine seriously.
- Healers are stepping forward, refusing to stay in the shadows.

The **Philippine Cannabinoid Network**, advocacy pages, support groups for epilepsy and chronic illness — these are not just modern groups.
They are **echoes of something ancient**.

And in those echoes, we hear the babaylan's voice again.

🌿 This Plant Has Always Been Ours

Cannabis isn't a Western invention.
It isn't a modern trend.

It is **indigenous**, **ancestral**, and **deeply Filipino**.

It belongs to:

- The Cordilleran farmer who never stopped planting
- The healer from Samar who keeps a prayer leaf in her wallet
- The grandmother in Sorsogon who says "nakakatulog lang ako pag meron niyan"

We don't need to *introduce* cannabis to the Philippines.
We need to **reintroduce the Philippines to its own past.**

This isn't about legalization alone.
It's about *liberation* — from stigma, from colonized thinking, from unjust laws.

🗨 **"Healing Was Never a Crime. Forgetting Was."**

Let's end this chapter not with facts — but with fire.

🌿 **Cannabis is not new. Criminalizing it is.**

🌿 **Babaylans were silenced, but their knowledge survived.**

🌿 **Your lola's tea, your tatay's back pain remedy — they weren't wrong. They were just early.**

We were a healing people long before we were a punished people.

Let's reclaim that title.

Let's bring healing back into the light — where it always belonged.

Chapter 5: The Global Awakening

"While we were taught to fear it, other nations learned to heal with it."

🌐 From Global Fear to Global Healing

For most of the 20th century, cannabis was treated like the villain of modern civilization.
A plant hunted by governments, feared by parents, and associated with crime, madness, and ruin.

That was the script.
And like many colonized nations, **the Philippines followed it blindly.**

But while we clung to outdated fears, something began to shift elsewhere in the world.

First in whispers.
Then in science.
Then in laws.

Today, cannabis is no longer a symbol of destruction — in many places, it is now a sign of progress, compassion, and innovation.

This is the **Global Awakening.**
And it's not just political — it's spiritual. Medical. Economic. Cultural.

The question now is simple:

Will we wake up — or get left behind?

TH Thailand: Southeast Asia's Gamechanger

Let's start close to home.

In a region known for strict anti-drug laws and zero-tolerance policies, one country dared to challenge the system: **Thailand.**

A decade ago, Thailand still had some of the harshest drug laws in Asia — long prison terms, even the **death penalty** for trafficking. Cannabis was lumped in with heroin and meth. The stigma was heavy.

But in **2018**, things changed.
Thailand **legalized medical cannabis**, making it the **first country in Southeast Asia** to do so.

Then in **2022**, it went further: **full decriminalization.**

Suddenly, the same plant once feared became a **national opportunity**.

What happened next?

- 🌱 **Farmers planted cannabis like rice**, creating new income streams.
- 🏪 Over **10,000 dispensaries opened**, legally licensed and regulated.
- 🌍 **Cannabis tourism exploded** — with travelers from around the world visiting for health, curiosity, and wellness.
- 💊 **Patients finally accessed relief** — including cancer patients, epileptics, PTSD sufferers, and more.

The sky didn't fall.
In fact, the country soared.

By 2023, Thailand's cannabis industry was worth over **$1.2 billion USD**, with projections to double within five years.

Thailand's approach wasn't perfect. Some policies were revised.
Some confusion followed.
But they did something brave — **they tried.**

They trusted their farmers.
They trusted their healers.
They trusted their people.

And now they're reaping the rewards.

US United States: From War on Drugs to Trillion-Dollar Transformation

The United States was once the global architect of anti-cannabis hysteria.

It launched the infamous **"War on Drugs"** in the 1970s — a campaign that led to mass incarceration, racial injustice, and billions spent on arrests and raids.
At its peak, America imprisoned more people for cannabis than any other country.

But over time — the truth began to crack through.

- Mothers of children with epilepsy came forward.
- Veterans spoke about cannabis helping PTSD.
- Doctors and researchers challenged the lies.
- Patients demanded access.

And the tide turned.

As of 2025:

- ☑ **38 U.S. states** allow **medical cannabis.**
- ☑ **24 states** have **full recreational legalization.**
- ☑ **Over 4 million** Americans are **registered patients.**
- 💰 The legal cannabis industry is worth **$35+ billion** — with **over 428,000 jobs** created.

States like **California, Oregon, Colorado, and New York** have become **models of regulated freedom** — offering lab-tested products, tax revenue, and safer options than the black market.

And here's the twist:

The same country that once pushed global prohibition…
…is now exporting **legal cannabis technology, research, and influence** around the world.

From criminal to corporate. From prison to prescription.

The U.S. proves: **healing can win — even after decades of harm.**

DECAUY Germany, Canada, Uruguay: Leadership Across Borders

CA Canada (Legal Since 2018)

- Became the **second country in the world** to fully legalize cannabis for adults.
- Today, Canada leads in:
  - International cannabis exports
  - Public education programs
  - Government-monitored cannabis research
- Health Canada strictly regulates quality and access — ensuring medical and recreational use are **safe and sustainable**.

UY Uruguay (The First Nation to Legalize, 2013)

- Small in size, massive in courage.
- Uruguay became the **first country in the world** to fully legalize and regulate cannabis.

- Government-controlled production ensured **equity and safety**.
- Despite international criticism, **Uruguay proved that moral leadership beats fear.**

DE Germany (Recreational Legalization in 2024)

- The **first major EU country** to go fully legal for recreational use.
- Created a public health-centered approach:
    - Decriminalization of small amounts
    - Education over incarceration
    - Home cultivation allowed
- Signals a huge shift in Europe, where more countries are now following suit.

PH The Philippines: Still Stuck in the Past?

While other nations evolve, **the Philippines remains frozen** — not because of science, but because of **stigma and politics**.

Here's the truth:

- 🚫 **Cannabis is still classified as a Schedule 1 dangerous drug.**
- 🧠 **Zero recorded deaths** from cannabis overdose — yet it remains feared.
- 🏥 Patients who could benefit — cancer fighters, trauma survivors, epileptics — **suffer in silence.**
- 🚔 Police continue to arrest poor users, while **black markets and smugglers thrive.**

- Filipino farmers — who could lead in organic cannabis cultivation — are **denied billions in potential income.**

We have the sun.
We have the soil.
We have the need.
But not yet — the courage.

This is not just sad.
It is **unjust**.

Signs of Change Are Flickering

Still, **hope isn't dead.**

The movement for medical cannabis in the Philippines is **gaining momentum** — slowly but surely:

- The **Medical Cannabis Compassionate Access Bill** has been filed in Congress multiple times.
- Advocacy groups like *Cannahopefuls*, *PCCS*, *PhilCann*, and others are **educating the public**, lobbying lawmakers, and **changing minds.**
- More doctors, researchers, and lawyers are stepping forward with **evidence, not fear**.
- Young Filipinos are more informed, curious, and **less afraid** of the word "weed."
- Some farmers are already **secretly cultivating** cannabis — risking jail just to help their communities.

The flame is small — but it's burning.

What it needs now is **oxygen**:
Awareness. Legislation. Political will. Public pressure.

✊ Global Doesn't Mean Foreign — It Means Possible

This isn't about copying Thailand, the U.S., or Canada blindly.
This is about realizing:

- 🌿 Healing is not owned by one nation.
- 🌿 Freedom is not exclusive.
- 🌿 And dignity is not foreign.

What the global awakening teaches us is **not who to follow — but what's possible.**

If a Buddhist country with death penalties can decriminalize...
If a Western superpower once obsessed with drug wars can evolve...
If tiny Uruguay can lead giants...

So can we.

We don't need to ask permission from history.
We need to **write our own version** of it.

🌍 The World Is Legalizing Healing.

The question now is simple:

Will the Philippines **lead**, **follow**, or **get left behind**?

This isn't just a global shift.
This is a **global calling**.

The world is choosing compassion over control.
Science over superstition.
Healing over punishment.

The only thing illegal now... is **ignoring the truth.**

Chapter 6: Breaking the Silence

"When truth is outlawed, only the brave speak."

There's a moment in every movement when the fear begins to crack. When whispers become voices. When silence becomes unbearable.

In the Philippines, that moment is arriving. Not through headlines or legislation just yet — but through the trembling voices of those once too afraid to speak. In provinces, in barbershops, in classrooms, online forums, and among families. The conversation is changing. Slowly. Unevenly. But undeniably.

This chapter isn't just about cannabis. It's about fear. It's about courage. It's about the tension between what is true and what is permitted to be said.

The High Price of Silence

For decades, cannabis has been wrapped in silence. Silence enforced by law. By stigma. By religion. By tradition. But silence comes at a cost.

Every patient who suffers in secret, every parent who watches their child seize because medicine is illegal, every farmer jailed while their crops are sold legally abroad — all pay the price.

They pay in pain. In poverty. In broken families. In lost futures.

To break the silence is to reclaim power. To say: "This is happening. This is real. And we will not be quiet anymore."

The Underground Movement

Across the archipelago, a quiet resistance is growing. • Students who write essays challenging anti-cannabis laws. • Nurses who whisper alternatives to dying patients. • Mothers who share CBD vials through hidden networks. • Elders who pass down stories of natural healing long before criminalization.

They're not forming protests with megaphones. Not yet. But they're creating space — in minds, in homes, in hearts. That space is where the law will eventually be rewritten.

Cannabis users are not shouting for attention. They're asking to be heard. And their stories — small, intimate, and brave — are the foundation of something bigger.

From Shame to Strength

One of the most powerful tools of oppression is shame. "You're an addict." "You're immoral." "You deserve this."

These labels stick. They isolate. They paralyze. But when people begin to say: "I'm not a criminal — I'm a father." "I'm not an addict — I'm a patient." "I'm not broken — I'm healing."

That's when the power shifts. Shame is replaced by dignity. And dignity demands rights.

Whispers from the Inside

Many who have spoken up paid the price. • A barangay health worker in Samar lost her job for talking about cannabis treatment. • A teacher in Ilocos was investigated for her student research project on cannabis and mental health. • An NGO volunteer was red-tagged and surveilled after hosting an information forum in Cebu.

But even with consequences, the silence keeps breaking. They understand something powerful: You don't need to be loud to be dangerous — you just need to be right.

Faith and Cannabis: Strange Allies?

One of the most complex intersections in the cannabis conversation is religion. Churches often condemn it. Sermons label it a sin. Believers avoid the topic entirely.

But some are starting to ask: What if God gave us this plant not as temptation — but as a gift?

In provinces, some priests and pastors quietly bless patients using herbal alternatives. They say: "Mercy is greater than law."

Some even cite scripture: "The leaves of the tree were for the healing of the nations." — Revelation 22:2

This reframe isn't just spiritual. It's political. Because when the church begins to question prohibition, politicians lose one of their strongest weapons: fear disguised as faith.

Youth: The Silence Breakers

If you want to see the future of this movement, look to the youth. TikTok creators sharing cannabis education. Poets writing about the war on drugs. Campus debaters tearing down outdated policies.

They're not afraid the way previous generations were. They've seen the science. The injustice. The global shift. They know that the war on drugs was never really a war on drugs — it was a war on the poor.

And they're not buying the old script. They're writing a new one.

Why Breaking Silence Matters

Every movement for justice started with people telling the truth — even when it was dangerous. • The LGBTQ+ rights movement. • Martial Law resistance. • The fight for press freedom.

Cannabis decriminalization is no different.

It begins with voices. With risk. With courage. Not because it's easy — but because the silence has become unbearable.

This Is Not Just a Trend

Some people think cannabis advocacy is just another online trend. A wave. A phase. They're wrong.

This is about health. About ancestral knowledge. About sovereignty.

It's about giving the poor what the rich already have access to — freedom to choose their healing.

It's not a phase. It's a return. To truth. To compassion. To balance.

To the Silent Ones Still Waiting

Maybe you're reading this, and you haven't spoken yet. Maybe you're a patient. A sibling. A friend. A believer. A farmer. Maybe you've been quiet because it felt safer.

That's okay.

But know this: you are not alone.

And when you're ready to speak — whether with a whisper, a song, a social post, or a march — your voice will matter. Because it adds weight to the truth.

And eventually, truth outweighs fear.

📣 The silence is cracking. And what breaks through — might heal us all.

Chapter 7: Criminalized but Not Criminals

"In this war, the poor bleed first. The sick get locked up. The rest just stay quiet."

In the Philippines, it doesn't take much to be labeled a "criminal."

A stick. A bottle cap. A dried leaf. A whisper.

Sometimes it's just a sick body looking for relief.

Other times, it's poverty daring to survive.

And in this country, those two things are more illegal than corruption.

This isn't just about cannabis anymore.
This is about who gets punished. Who gets protected.
And who gets erased.

The law doesn't always chase crime. Sometimes, it manufactures it.

A Mother in the Mountains

She lived in a remote sitio in Northern Luzon. No electricity. No pharmacy. Just soil and sky.

Her son was seven when the seizures began. They would strike in the middle of the night — his body stiff, mouth foaming, eyes rolling into the dark. She held him, prayed, begged the wind for mercy.

The government gave none.

She had no PhilHealth. No neurologist. No jeepney fare to the next town.

A neighbor — an old woman who still believed in leaves and spirits — handed her a few dried buds.

"Subukan mo lang. Hindi ito masama. Matagal na 'to sa atin."

She boiled it into tea.

That night, her son slept.

It wasn't a cure. But it was a start.

Then the barangay tanod found out.

She was reported, arrested, and paraded barefoot down a gravel road as if she were some cartel queenpin.

There was no lawyer. No bail. No headlines.

Now she sits in a jail two towns away, her case forgotten like so many others — just another "pusher" in the system's eyes.

But in her heart, she's still a mother.
Still fighting.
Still praying that someone, somewhere, remembers her name.

A Father in the Slums

He once built the city's skyline — carrying steel on his shoulders, mixing cement, sweating dreams into high-rise towers he could never afford to live in.

Then he fell. A cracked spine ended his job, and with it, his income.

Painkillers were too expensive. Alcohol made things worse.

So he turned to a small roll of dry relief — a joint passed discreetly between calloused hands in a dark alley.

It helped him sleep. Helped him move.

But it also made him a target.

He was caught during a buy-bust.

Dragged out like a murderer. Pinned down. Cuffed.

His wife screamed. His children cried. The barangay watched like it was a show.

The headlines didn't mention his back. Or his kids. Or the decades he spent building malls and bridges.

They only called him a "drug suspect."

That was all it took to erase his humanity.

Addict. Pusher. Junkie. Criminal.

The labels come fast. And once they're stuck to your name, they stain everything.

These words are weapons — crafted to silence sympathy, simplify judgment, and keep the cycle moving.

But here's the deeper truth:

- **Not everyone who uses is broken.**
- **Not everyone who's caught is guilty.**
- **And not everyone who profits from this war gets caught at all.**

The ones moving tons of shabu through shipping containers? Protected.

The ones growing five plants in the mountains for epilepsy treatment? Persecuted.

Welcome to the Philippines — where the line between crime and survival is drawn in privilege.

The Numbers Don't Lie — They Bleed

📊 Over 70,000 drug-related arrests happen in the Philippines every year.
📊 The vast majority involve users, not traffickers.
📊 Most are poor — informal workers, tricycle drivers, farmers, unemployed youth.
📊 Bail ranges from ₱200,000 to ₱500,000 for possession cases — unreachable for most.
📊 Some people spend 7 to 10 years in jail before even seeing trial.

And yet, the government says this is justice.

But what it really is… is mass punishment.

This isn't a "war on drugs." It's a war on the margins.

On the ones with no lawyers. No money. No media coverage.

The same system that lets drug lords sponsor barangay fiestas — jails a mother for two grams.

The same system that praises compassion in Senate speeches — lets detainees rot without trial.

Pain Is Not a Crime

There are people in jail right now who:

- Just wanted to sleep without shaking.
- Needed relief from terminal cancer.
- Were too poor to afford branded medications.
- Smoked to calm trauma, not to chase a high.

They are not threats to society.

They are victims of a system that criminalizes healing.

And when healing becomes illegal —
The law is the disease.

Generational Injustice

When a parent is jailed for cannabis...

- Their kids drop out of school.
- Families break apart.
- Shame infects every aspect of life.

Children grow up hating their own bloodline, taught to believe their mother or father was evil — not because they were, but because the state said so.

And these children? They grow up with trauma, poverty, and no trust in institutions.

They become the next targets.

The cycle feeds itself.

And the war lives on — long after the smoke clears.

The Rich Use It Too. But They Don't Get Raided.

Make no mistake: cannabis isn't exclusive to the slums.

You'll find it in private condos. Luxury resorts. CEO yachts.

You just won't find SWAT teams bursting through their doors.

The rich can hire doctors to write foreign prescriptions.

They can fly to California, Thailand, or Amsterdam.

They can "medicate" in peace.

But the poor? They light a joint — and end up on a body count.

That's not law enforcement.
That's social control.

The Real Crime Is Silence

Every time we ignore those rotting in jail for trying to survive…

Every time we laugh at a "stoner" meme while someone's daughter waits in court…

Every time we believe headlines without asking what came before the arrest…

We become accomplices.

Because cannabis has victims in the Philippines — but not because of the plant.

Because of the policy.
Because of the silence.
Because of the refusal to listen.

What If It Was You?

Ask yourself:

- If your child had seizures and nothing else worked, would you break the law?
- If your parent had cancer and was dying in pain, would you boil the leaves?
- If your body ached every night and all you had was a joint — would you risk it?

Because thousands of Filipinos have answered "Yes."

And for that, they were jailed. Labeled. Forgotten.

Not because they're criminals — but because the law lacks compassion.

◎ Let's See Them Again.

Let's bring them back from the shadows.

- The grandfather rubbing oil on his knees.
- The mother mixing tea for seizures.
- The teacher hiding CBD in a vitamin bottle.
- The tricycle driver clutching hope under his seat.

They are not enemies.

They are proof.

Proof that our laws are not just outdated —
They are unjust.

This Is Not a Call to Chaos. It's a Call to Humanity.

We are not saying legalize recklessly.
We are saying — stop punishing people for trying to live.

We are saying — regulate, educate, and protect.
Not raid, shame, and destroy.

🚫 Cannabis has victims in the Philippines.

🧬 Not because of addiction.

🌿 Not because of danger.

⚖️ But because we forgot the difference between a crime and a crisis.

It's time to remember.

It's time to choose justice over judgment.

It's time to decriminalize compassion.

Chapter 8: Science, Not Fear

"They told us to be afraid. But the science? It tells a different story."

For generations, the word *cannabis* didn't mean a plant — it meant punishment.

It meant:

- "Your son's a failure."
- "Your daughter's a delinquent."
- "You'll never get hired."
- "You'll ruin your life."

It meant shame.

From classrooms to courtrooms, we were taught to fear it.

They said it melts your brain. Turns you lazy. Destroys futures.

No questions. Just slogans.

But here's the thing about fear: it's loud when facts are missing.

And now?

The facts are here.

Zero Deaths. Let That Sink In.

Let's start with what no one expected to be true:

Cannabis has never caused a fatal overdose.

Not once. Not in centuries of use. Not in any medical journal. Not even in the mountains or inner cities where it's used most often.

Compare that to:

- 🚬 **Tobacco** — Kills **8 million people** per year. (WHO)
- 🍺 **Alcohol** — Kills **3 million** annually.
- 💊 **Paracetamol (Biogesic)** — Leads to thousands of accidental overdoses and liver damage cases every year.
- 🌿 **Cannabis? – Zero overdose deaths. Ever.**

Let that land.

The legal killers are in every sari-sari store. The deadly drinks are in every mall. But the plant that's *never* killed anyone?

That one will get you 12 years in prison.

Does that sound like justice — or a system scared of the truth?

The Endocannabinoid System: Built to Receive

Here's what school never taught us:

Every human body has an internal system called the **endocannabinoid system (ECS)** — and it was only discovered in the 1990s.

This system is responsible for regulating:

- Pain
- Mood
- Appetite
- Memory
- Sleep

- Immune function
- Inflammation response

In short, the ECS keeps your body in balance.

And cannabis? It fits right into this system — like a key fits a lock.

🌿 **THC** and **CBD**, the two main compounds in cannabis, **bind naturally** to cannabinoid receptors in the brain and body. They're not foreign invaders. They're partners.

That's not witchcraft.
That's **biology**.

That's why cannabis helps with so many conditions — because the body is *built* to interact with it.

Why didn't they teach us that?

Real Science. Real Healing.

Let's drop the street myths and tabloid noise.

Here's what **peer-reviewed** science — global and local — actually says about medical cannabis:

🔬 **Chronic Pain Relief**
Cannabis helps with neuropathic pain, arthritis, cancer pain, and fibromyalgia. In many studies, it's more effective (and safer) than opioids.

🧠 **Epilepsy & Seizures**
CBD-based medications like **Epidiolex** are **FDA-approved** in the U.S. They've helped children with rare forms of epilepsy go from 300 seizures a week to almost none.

💥 **PTSD & Anxiety**
Veterans. Abuse survivors. Disaster victims. All report reduced

nightmares, flashbacks, and panic when using controlled cannabis treatment.

Multiple Sclerosis (MS)
Cannabis helps reduce muscle spasms, stiffness, and nerve pain in MS patients.

Glaucoma
Cannabis lowers intraocular pressure — the main cause of blindness in glaucoma.

Appetite & Nausea
Especially useful for chemotherapy patients and those with HIV/AIDS. It brings back appetite and eases vomiting.

And more conditions are being studied every year — Alzheimer's, Parkinson's, Crohn's disease, and even some types of cancer.

This isn't fantasy.

It's fact. It's science.
And it's being buried under old laws and older fears.

No, It Doesn't "Melt" the Brain

One of the oldest scare tactics?

"Weed kills brain cells."

But where's the evidence?

Nowhere.

Modern research has **debunked** this repeatedly.

Some studies even suggest that **CBD may protect the brain** from trauma, stroke damage, and inflammation.

Yes — **protect**, not destroy.

Is it harmless? No. Heavy, frequent use in teenagers (whose brains are still developing) **can** affect short-term memory and concentration.

But that's not "brain rot."

That's moderation. That's context. That's parenting and education — not prohibition.

Let's stop punishing adults for what teenagers might do.

Even the Global Authorities Changed Their Minds

Let's talk about what the *world* is saying now:

🌍 **The United Nations (UN)**
In 2020, cannabis was removed from **Schedule IV** — the list of the most dangerous drugs with no medical use. This is the same list where heroin sits.

They finally admitted: Cannabis has **legitimate medical value**.

🌍 **The World Health Organization (WHO)**
Recommends cannabis for multiple conditions, and has called for **more research, not criminalization**.

US **The U.S. Government**
Holds **Patent #6630507** — for cannabinoids as **neuroprotectants and antioxidants**.

That's right: The same government that criminalized cannabis also **patented its healing power.**

Let that contradiction sit with you for a moment.

If even the system that banned it now profits from its science — how long will we let fear blind us?

But Isn't Cannabis Addictive?

Let's be honest.

Yes — **cannabis can be habit-forming.**

About 1 in 10 users may develop some form of dependence — usually with heavy, daily use.

But here's the bigger picture:

- 🍺 **Alcohol addiction rate:** 1 in 7
- 🚬 **Tobacco addiction rate:** 1 in 3
- 📱 **Social media & gaming addiction?** Rising fast, with no regulation.
- 🍩 **Sugar?** Linked to obesity, heart disease, diabetes — and addictive as hell.

So why the double standard?

Why is cannabis feared more than substances that **actually kill** and **actually ruin lives**?

Let's stop pretending the plant is the problem.

The problem is **how we treat the plant.**

Philippine Science Is Ready — If We Let It Breathe

You know who wants to study cannabis?

Not just hippies.

- Doctors at **PGH**
- Researchers at **UP Diliman, UP Manila, and DLSU**
- Agricultural scientists in Bukidnon, Baguio, and Davao
- DOH employees who see suffering every day but can't speak out

- Rural health workers who've seen cannabis help patients when nothing else could

But they can't move.
Because the law keeps them frozen.

No funding.
No permissions.
No protection.

Fear blocks research.
Ignorance blocks legislation.
Stigma blocks truth.

We have the brains.
We just need the **freedom to ask questions.**

Why Did They Lie?

Maybe it was control.

Maybe it was ignorance.

Maybe it was colonial legacy. (The U.S. brought the cannabis ban here in 1961 — before Filipino scientists could even study it.)

But the result is the same:

Decades of fear.
Hundreds of thousands arrested.
Millions misinformed.
Billions wasted on punishment instead of healing.

Isn't it time we rewrite that story?

🧬 Science Doesn't Fear the Plant. Only People Do.

Let's make it plain:

Cannabis is **not a miracle.**

It's not a "one-size-fits-all" cure.

It's not perfect.

But it is:

☑ Safer than alcohol or tobacco
☑ Biologically compatible with our bodies
☑ Scientifically supported for dozens of conditions
☑ A source of hope for millions in pain

And most of all — it's **not the enemy.**

Fear is.

📖 The Truth Is Speaking. Are We Ready to Listen?

This war on cannabis isn't just a war on a plant.
It's a war on science.
A war on logic.
A war on progress.

But wars end.

And when they do, **truth remains.**

So let's choose:

🔬 Not fear.
🗞 Not propaganda.
🌱 But knowledge.
🧠 But science.
❤️ But compassion.

Because *when fear fades, healing begins.*

Chapter 9: Lies We Were Told

"Before they locked us up, they brainwashed us first."

For most Filipinos, fear of cannabis wasn't rooted in reality.

It wasn't a personal encounter with the plant.

It wasn't because someone smoked and attacked them, or because they saw a friend's life destroyed by weed.

No.

It came from something else:

- 📺 A 5-minute school lecture.
- 📰 A screaming news headline.
- ⛪ A fire-and-brimstone sermon at Sunday Mass.
- 🧓 "Sabi nila…" — from a parent or barangay elder, often just passing down what *they* were told.

And just like that, a plant that predates our constitution by thousands of years — even predates *Christianity* — became a villain in our national story.

But if you dig deep enough — beneath the news, the laws, the fear — you find a disturbing pattern.

A deliberate one.

We weren't protected from cannabis. We were programmed to fear it.

And the worst part?

We were lied to.

Over and over.

Lie #1: Cannabis is a Gateway Drug

"Start with weed, end with shabu."

It's the first thing you hear in any anti-drug seminar. Like some sort of cursed ladder — one puff of cannabis and suddenly you're breaking into houses, cooking meth, dying in alleys.

But here's what science — not slogans — actually says:

- **Most cannabis users never go on to use "hard drugs."**
- **In fact, many people try alcohol, nicotine, or even prescription drugs first.**
- **The real gateways?** Poverty. Trauma. Mental illness. Unhealed pain.

Addiction isn't caused by cannabis.
It's caused by **disconnection** — from family, from purpose, from support.

And yet, we never called alcohol a "gateway." We never demonized cigarettes. Those got clever marketing and tax stamps.

Cannabis got handcuffs.

Why?

Because this lie wasn't about truth.

It was about **control**.

Lie #2: It Has No Medical Use

Ask any lola or lolo in the provinces.

They'll tell you:

"Ginagamit namin 'yan dati. Pampakalma. Pampatulog. Pampawala ng sakit sa katawan."

Long before hospitals, Filipinos were using plants. Cannabis included.

In fact, **Spanish colonizers documented** its use as early as **1521** — centuries before any pharma company touched Philippine soil.

So what happened?

Where did the "no medical use" argument come from?

📍 **The U.S. — 1930s.**

A man named **Harry Anslinger**, head of America's Federal Bureau of Narcotics, needed a new enemy to keep his budget alive after alcohol prohibition ended.

He found one: **cannabis**.

And how did he sell the fear?

- **Racism:** "It makes Black men lust after white women."
- **Xenophobia:** "It makes Mexican immigrants violent."
- **Fake science:** "It leads to insanity and murder."
- **Hollywood:** Films like *Reefer Madness* showing young people going psychotic after one puff.

The Philippines, being a U.S. colony at the time, inherited that fear — no questions asked.

Their war became our law.

Their propaganda became our education.

Their racism became our religion.

Lie #3: Cannabis Makes You Crazy

"Pag nag-weed ka, sisira utak mo."

Sound familiar?

It was probably said by a teacher, a neighbor, or a classmate parroting what they heard from TV.

But is it true?

Not quite.

Here's what actual research says:

- **Cannabis can influence mood**, especially in high doses — just like **caffeine**, **alcohol**, or even **lack of sleep**.
- It **can** worsen symptoms for people already struggling with schizophrenia or bipolar disorder.
- But for many others, cannabis — especially in controlled amounts — can **reduce anxiety**, **ease PTSD**, and even **lift depression**.

Some studies suggest cannabis promotes **neurogenesis** (growth of new brain cells), especially **CBD**.

So, does cannabis make everyone crazy?

No.

But telling everyone that it does?

That keeps people obedient.
Scared.
Afraid to question.
Afraid to try.

Because fear keeps the system intact.

And **truth** makes people think — and that's dangerous.

Lie #4: It's Just for Tambays and Addicts

This one is crueler than most — because it shames people into silence.

The typical image?

A shirtless man.
Smoking on the kanto.
Doing "nothing with his life."

But let's widen the lens.

Around the world, cannabis is used by:

- **Artists** for inspiration
- **CEOs** to manage stress
- **Veterans** to heal trauma
- **Doctors** to treat patients (and sometimes themselves)
- **Farmers** who grow it for livelihood
- **Parents** with cancer, epilepsy, chronic pain
- **Musicians** who changed culture (Bob Marley, The Beatles, Snoop Dogg, Lady Gaga)

Even **President Duterte** — yes, the man behind the deadliest drug war in Asia — once admitted:

"I use marijuana to stay awake."

The lie wasn't really about cannabis.
It was about **classism**.

Rich people were "creative."
Poor people were "tambay."
Same plant. Different labels. Different punishment.

That's not justice.
That's a system trying to stay in power.

Lie #5: It's Against God

Churches love to say:

"Your body is a temple. Don't defile it with drugs."

Fair.

But they never say that about pork, Coke, or cigarettes — all of which damage the body, too.

Let's talk Bible:

- The Bible **never mentions cannabis** — not once.
- Some scholars believe the **"kaneh-bosm"** listed in the **anointing oil** of Exodus may have referred to cannabis or a related plant.
- Across ancient cultures — **Africa, India, China, Persia, and even the Middle East** — cannabis was used as **medicine** and **spiritual aid**.
- In the Philippines, babaylans and albularyos used it for generations before Western religion erased those practices.

So who said it was "evil"?

Not Jesus.
Not science.

But **colonizers**, **missionaries**, and **governments** — the same forces that burned herbal books and replaced them with imported pills and foreign sermons.

Why They Lied

The answer is simple — and brutal:

Because scared people are easier to control.

Because when you're afraid of healing yourself, you'll keep buying what they sell.

Because imprisoning poor Filipinos for a plant is easier than fixing poverty, trauma, or broken systems.

Because **fear wins elections.**
Because **the media repeats whatever keeps ratings high.**

We grew up with:

- 🚨 "DRUG USER ARRESTED!"
- 💀 "DRUG PUSHER KILLED!"
- 😱 "DRUG RAID IN BARANGAY!"

But we were never asked:

What drug?
How much?
Why was he using it?
Did he hurt anyone?

We weren't told to ask.

We were told to obey.

📺 The Lies Killed More Than the Plant Ever Did

The war on cannabis didn't just arrest people.

It:

- Broke families.
- Destroyed futures.

- Filled jails with non-violent "criminals."
- Blocked research.
- Silenced doctors.
- Kept sick people from relief.
- Killed dreams before they could begin.

While cigarettes still advertise on highways.

While liquor flows at every birthday party.

While sugar, gambling, and gossip rot us from the inside — legally.

And now?

Now we're finally starting to ask questions.

🧠 It's Not Just a Plant. It's a Mirror.

Cannabis isn't just about medicine or recreation.

It's a mirror.

It reflects:

- How we treat the poor.
- How we value truth.
- How we allow systems to control what we're allowed to heal with, think about, or believe in.

It shows us that **the real addiction** may not be to weed — but to **punishment**, **fear**, and **obedience**.

So it's time we ask:

- Who benefits from the lie?
- Who profits from the fear?

- And what happens when we finally see the truth?

📖 *Because truth heals — and lies divide.*

📢 *And if we don't challenge the lies, we become part of them.*

Chapter 10: What Legalization Could Look Like

"Imagine a Philippines where healing isn't a crime."

We've unpacked the lies.

We've heard the silenced voices.
We've felt the weight of policies not written for us.
We've seen other countries take bold steps forward — not out of recklessness, but out of reason, compassion, and truth.

Now it's our turn.

Legalization in the Philippines doesn't have to be wild or out-of-control.
It doesn't have to mimic the mistakes of others.
It doesn't even have to be flashy.

It can be calm.
It can be wise.
It can be deeply Filipino.

We are not trying to "import" a movement.
We are simply trying to remember what was once ours — **a sacred relationship with a healing plant.**

So what could a post-prohibition Philippines look like?

Here's a vision — not a fantasy — of a nation that chose healing over fear.

---

1. Medical First — With Compassion and Clarity

PH A medical cannabis program rooted in empathy, not red tape.

Let's begin where the need is most urgent: the sick, the suffering, and the silenced.

Picture this:

- A **young girl with epilepsy** in Iloilo no longer begging her parents to risk jail just to ease her seizures.
- A **father with late-stage cancer** in Davao finally able to sleep through the night without pain.
- A **veteran with PTSD** from Marawi walking into a clinic, not a prison.

We can build a system where:

- Patients can **access cannabis through licensed doctors**, not street pushers.
- Local **physicians are trained and certified** to recommend safe treatment.
- **Compassion centers** are established in hospitals, barangays, and public health units.
- **Medicinal products** (oils, capsules, teas) are tested, labeled, and regulated for dosage and purity.

This isn't radical.
It's responsible.

We've done it with antibiotics, with insulin, with morphine — all substances that can heal or harm depending on access and regulation.

It's time we **treat cannabis like the medicine it is** — and protect those who need it most.

Because **no Filipino should have to choose between jail and relief**.

2. Farmers First — Empowering the Roots

🌿 We start at the soil — where the real power lives.

Imagine this:

- A **cooperative in Bukidnon** training farmers on organic cannabis cultivation.
- A **barangay in Benguet** exporting high-quality hemp fiber for clothing, paper, and packaging.
- A **livelihood center in Mindoro** creating CBD tinctures for local clinics.

The potential is enormous.

Here's how we get it right:

- **Only Filipino farmers** — not foreign conglomerates — get first rights to cultivation.
- Establish **government-supported grower cooperatives** for licensing, education, and tools.
- Offer **technical training** on sustainable growing, pest control, and soil regeneration.
- Partner with **UP Los Baños, Visayas State University**, and other agri-tech schools for R&D.

We already subsidize rice, corn, and sugar.

Why not invest in a plant that heals people and the planet?

This isn't just about business.
It's about **reclaiming sovereignty over our land and labor.**

We don't need outsiders to "bring us cannabis."

We've had it all along.

---

3. Jobs. Business. Innovation.

Let's be clear:

Cannabis is not just a plant.

It's a **multi-billion peso industry** waiting to bloom — in ways that align with our values and culture.

In a legalized future:

- 🌱 **Startups** create local CBD oils, body balms, capsules, and herbal blends.
- ☕ **Cafés and spas** offer calming cannabis-infused teas and massage oils — especially for senior citizens and OFW retirees.
- 🧬 **Laboratories and universities** run research on cannabinoid science.
- 📦 **Packaging companies** pivot to hemp-based materials — biodegradable and eco-friendly.
- 📲 **Digital platforms** build delivery systems, traceability apps, and farmer-to-patient networks.

Every step of this ecosystem creates:

- **Jobs** — not just in cultivation, but also marketing, logistics, IT, retail, legal, design, and analytics.
- **Entrepreneurship** — for local inventors, healers, and communities often excluded from traditional capital.
- **Tourism** — imagine a "healing trail" from La Union to Siargao, offering wellness retreats and cannabis education tours.

We missed the wave on semiconductors.
We're playing catch-up on AI.
But cannabis?

This wave hasn't passed.
And we could lead it — the Filipino way.

---

4. Regulation, Not Chaos

Critics always say:

"But what if people abuse it?"
"What if it gets out of control?"
"What if teens get access?"

Valid concerns.

But **legalization doesn't mean lawlessness**.

It means building a better system — one that is **transparent, fair, and enforceable**.

A functional framework includes:

- **Age restrictions** — 21 and up only, just like alcohol or tobacco.
- **Product testing** — to ensure purity, dosage accuracy, and no dangerous additives.
- **Taxation systems** — modeled on the sin tax, with cannabis funds earmarked for:
    - Public health
    - Mental health services
    - Drug rehabilitation (voluntary, not punitive)
    - Cannabis education programs
- **Licensing and compliance audits** — for growers, processors, and sellers.
- **Local community boards** — to approve dispensaries and prevent over-concentration.

- **Penalties** — for selling to minors, using in school zones, or distributing unregulated products.

We can even **geo-lock cannabis access by province**, starting with pilot areas like Baguio, Cebu, or Davao, then expanding once data confirms success.

Legalization doesn't mean losing control.
It means **taking control back** — from illegal markets and giving it to systems that work.

---

5. Restorative Justice — Free the Wrongfully Jailed

More than 6,000 Filipinos are behind bars for cannabis.

Some for a few grams.
Some for using it to treat illness.
Some because they were poor, brown, or in the wrong place at the wrong time.

If we legalize without releasing them, what message are we sending?

That the law was unjust — but only moving forward?

We must go back for those who were punished under the lie.

Legalization must include:

- **Immediate release** for those convicted of non-violent cannabis offenses.
- **Expungement of criminal records**, so they can work, vote, and rebuild.
- **Reintegration programs** offering therapy, job training, and housing.
- **Support for families** affected by incarceration.
- **Public apology and acknowledgment** of the injustice — not just in law, but in spirit.

This is not just policy.
It's humanity.

Because **we cannot heal as a nation while leaving our people in cages** for something that is no longer a crime.

---

6. A Cultural Reconnection

Cannabis was in our culture long before Christianity arrived.
Long before America's war on drugs.

It was **medicine**, **ritual**, and **relief**.

But colonization erased that memory.
Missionaries burned our botany books.
Politicians banned our plants.
And now? Most young Filipinos don't even know cannabis ever had a place in our roots.

Legalization is not just law.
It's **reconnection.**

We can:

- Celebrate **Philippine herbalism** — and integrate cannabis into **community healing** alongside lagundi, sambong, tawa-tawa, and more.
- Protect and uplift **indigenous plant wisdom** — and give our babaylans, albularyos, and hilots the space they deserve in the national health dialogue.
- Encourage **cultural festivals** that honor herbal traditions — not just for tourists, but for education.
- Develop **curricula** in schools that teach drug history with balance, truth, and critical thinking.

The goal is not to glorify cannabis.
It's to **remove the shame**, and **restore the dignity** of our healing traditions.

7. A Safer, Healthier Society

With legalization, society doesn't fall apart.

It gets stronger — *if* we do it right.

Here's what we gain:

- 🛑 **The black market collapses.** When people can access safe, legal cannabis, they stop buying from dangerous, unregulated sellers.
- 🚔 **Police resources are freed** — to pursue serious crimes like trafficking, abuse, and corruption.
- 🧠 **Public education** replaces fear with facts — especially among youth.
- 🩺 **More people seek help** for mental health without fear of being arrested.
- 💸 **Tax revenue funds schools and hospitals**, not foreign drug wars.
- 👨‍👩‍👧‍👦 **Families stay whole** — fewer parents locked up, fewer children orphaned by the justice system.

Legalization is not about being high.
It's about building a **higher-functioning** society.

Where wellness is prioritized.
Where facts matter.
Where no one is criminalized for healing.

"This Isn't a Dream — It's a Blueprint."

Thailand did it.
Germany did it.
Colombia, Canada, South Africa — all charted their own course.

And here we are — the Philippines — still waiting, still hesitating.

But what if we stopped?

What if we led?

What if we turned this leaf not just as policy — but as a nation that finally chose truth over fear?

Let's be clear:

- **Legalization is not a silver bullet.**
- **It won't fix everything overnight.**
- **But it starts something.**

It tells the sick: *"You deserve comfort."*
It tells farmers: *"You matter."*
It tells the poor: *"You are not disposable."*
It tells the future: *"We made a mistake — and we fixed it."*

This is not radical.

This is **responsible evolution**.

It's time we legalized cannabis — not because it's trendy, not because it's profitable, but because **it's the right thing to do**.

"And maybe, just maybe — when healing is no longer illegal — this nation will finally begin to heal itself."

Chapter 11: Lift The Stigma — The Movement

"Change doesn't start in Congress. It starts in the streets. In the stories. In the truth."

For decades, the cannabis conversation in the Philippines was not a conversation.

It was a **sermon. A warning. A war.**

They talked.
We listened.
They judged.
We stayed silent.

For too long, the loudest voices were those of fearmongers, moralists, and corrupted officials — not doctors, patients, or healers.
Not parents.
Not the people.

But not anymore.

The Silence Is Breaking. The Movement Is Rising.

Something is shifting.
Not just in law, but in energy.
Not just in policy, but in people.

What once was a whisper among friends…
Is now a conversation on campuses.
A chant in community centers.

A headline on local blogs.
A bold truth declared in daylight.

We're not hiding anymore.
We're **healing in public**.

Because **cannabis never needed saving.**
We did.

The Real Fight Was Never Against the Plant

Let's get honest.

This was never truly about a leaf.
This was never really about getting high.

The real fight was — and always has been — against:

- **Ignorance**
  A system that refuses to update its science.
- **Corruption**
  Officials who profit from punishment.
- **Fear**
  Pushed by institutions that gain power through control.
- **Oppression**
  A tool used to jail the poor while the rich walk free.
- **The Lie**
  That healing with a plant is more dangerous than dying without it.

The war on cannabis was never about health.
It was about **silencing an entire generation's potential to think, to heal, to rebel, to rise**.

And now we've seen through the smoke.
Now we know.

Who's Part of the Movement?

When people say "stoners" or "users," they try to reduce the complexity of this community into a lazy stereotype.

But **look closer.**

This movement is:

- A **mother** whose child needs cannabis to stop daily seizures.
- A **farmer** who wants to grow legally and finally rise from poverty.
- A **cancer survivor** who found peace in the plant after chemo broke his body.
- A **youth** who's tired of being demonized for asking *why*.
- A **healer** preserving ancient traditions.
- A **doctor** who risked her license to help a patient live.
- A **tattoo artist** who speaks through ink and pain.
- A **tricycle driver**, a **singer**, a **teacher**, a **soldier**, a **rapper**, a **rebel**, a **believer**...

This is not a niche.

This is the nation.

And anyone who recognizes that the war on weed was never a war on drugs —
it was a war on us —
is part of this movement.

What Does It Mean to "Lift the Stigma"?

To **lift the stigma** is not just to change a law — it's to change a mindset.

It means:

Speaking up
Telling your truth. Whether you're a patient, a grower, or just someone who believes in justice.

Organizing
Starting with a group chat, ending with a town hall. Hosting teach-ins, healing circles, peaceful marches.

Voting smart
Electing leaders who *listen*, who believe in science, who prioritize healing over handcuffs.

Educating with love
Especially our families. Not with anger. Not with rebellion. But with **truth, patience, and empathy**.

Building homegrown systems
Research. Data. Farming models. Clinical trials. Culturally rooted solutions made *by* Filipinos, *for* Filipinos.

Lifting the stigma means:

- We stop whispering when we talk about cannabis.
- We stop hiding it behind sarcasm or shame.
- We stop letting others define the narrative.

No One's Coming to Save Us — We Save Ourselves

Let's stop waiting.

- Not for Congress.
- Not for the DOH.
- Not for CNN Philippines.
- Not for American investors or celebrity endorsements.

Be the media.
Be the message.
Be the movement.

This is how real change begins:

1. One voice — quietly telling the truth.
2. Then two — comparing notes.
3. Then five — organizing a small meetup.
4. Then fifty — marching, writing, creating.
5. Then thousands — refusing to be silent.
6. Then the nation — transforming itself from the ground up.

It doesn't start with a Senate bill.

It starts with **you reading this book** — and deciding not to shut up.

✊ **"One voice can challenge a lie. A million voices can end it."**

You may feel small.
But your voice is powerful.

The same way they used lies to control a generation,
we can use truth to set the next one free.

Every meme.
Every post.
Every calm, confident conversation with your Lola, your barkada, your barangay captain…
is resistance.

And resistance is how every movement begins.

The Future Is Ours to Build

One day, your children might open a history book and read:

"In 2025, the Filipino people stood up.
They didn't wait for permission.
They lifted the truth.
They lifted their families.
They lifted each other.
They lifted the stigma."

Let that be your legacy.

So… What Now?

You've read the facts.
You've felt the fire.

Here's what to do next:

🔓 **Share this book**
Give it to a friend, a family member, a stranger. Start a dialogue.

🧠 **Question everything**
From drug laws to news headlines to what you were taught in school.

🌱 **Heal openly**
If you're using cannabis to manage pain or trauma — *you are not a criminal.* Don't carry that shame.

🔥 **Light the way**
Through art. Through music. Through medicine. Through movement.

Because the only thing more powerful than fear…

is us.

Lift the Stigma. Start the Movement.

This isn't the end.
This is the **beginning**.

Of a louder truth.
Of a healed generation.
Of a freer Philippines.

Let this book be the first chapter.
You will write the next ones.

And when people ask:

"What did you do during the movement?"

You'll smile and say:

"I lit the match."
"I broke the silence."
"I helped lift the stigma."

🔥 Mabuhay ang katotohanan. Mabuhay ang paghilom. Mabuhay ang kilusan.

The revolution is not tomorrow.
The revolution is now.

Acknowledgements

No one writes a book like this alone — not when it comes from pain, struggle, and truth.

First, I want to thank the people who lived this story before it was ever written — the patients, the farmers, the advocates, and even the wrongly accused. This book carries your voices. I hope I did you justice.

To the ones who stayed with me through the hardest nights, when life was messy and heavy — thank you for believing I had something worth saying.

To those who judged me, doubted me, or tried to silence me — thank you too. You gave me the fire I needed to finish this.

To the ancestors of this land — the albularyos, the healers, and the forgotten warriors who knew the value of plants and peace — your wisdom lives on in these pages.

To my children, — you are my reason. I dedicate this truth to your future.

To everyone who read this with an open heart — you are part of the movement now.

And to the higher force that kept me going when I had nothing left — you know who you are.

We rise because we remember.
We fight because we love.
We heal because we dare to speak.

Maraming salamat. This book is for all of us.
— Francis

About the Author

Francis Louie is a Filipino visionary, storyteller, father, and freedom-seeker born in Mindanao. With no big backing, no fancy degrees, and no privilege to stand on — just raw experience, street wisdom, and a heart burning with purpose — he decided to write the book that many were too afraid to.

Surrounded by struggle but guided by spirit, Francis turned pain into purpose and silence into a voice for the voiceless. His mission: to break the stigma, speak the truth, and help pave the way for healing and justice in the Philippines, especially for those who've been judged, locked up, or forgotten simply for surviving.

He believes that cannabis is not the enemy — corruption, ignorance, and injustice are. This book is part of something bigger than a debate about a plant — it's about a shift in consciousness. It's about fighting for truth, for the future, and for his children, your children, to grow up in a freer, wiser world.

Francis Louie writes not from a throne — but from the ground, with the people, for the people.

About the Publisher

This book was independently published under **LOUIEWOOD,** a grassroots imprint created to give voice to the silenced, light to the misunderstood, and power to those left out of the narrative. LOUIEWOOD isn't backed by corporations, politics, or big money — it's powered by truth, purpose, and the belief that stories like this can spark change.

Founded in Mindanao, Philippines, LOUIEWOOD exists to amplify raw, unfiltered voices from the ground. We publish not for profit, but for progress — for healing, justice, and freedom. Whether this book reaches one reader or a million, our mission stays the same: Expose the lies. Break the stigma. Light the path forward.

This is publishing for the people. This is the fight for the future.

Made in United States
North Haven, CT
05 November 2026

21765362R60049